AF271246

A good manager
doesn't try to eliminate conflict;
he tries to keep it
from wasting the energies of his people.

Robert Townsend

The Manager's
CONFLICT
RESOLUTION
Handbook

A Practical Guide for Creating Positive Change

Ilayne J. Geller & David Cottrell

The Manager's
CONFLICT
RESOLUTION
Handbook

Copyright © 2008 Ilayne J. Geller. All rights reserved.

No part of this book may be reproduced in any form without written permission in advance from the publisher. International rights and foreign translations available only through negotiation with CornerStone Leadership Institute.

Inquiries regarding permission for use of the material contained in this book should be addressed to:

CornerStone Leadership Institute
P.O. Box 764087
Dallas, TX 75376
888.789.LEAD

Printed in the United States of America
ISBN: 978-0-9798009-8-6

Credits

Editor   Juli Baldwin, The Baldwin Group, Dallas, TX
                                          Juli@BaldwinGrp.com

Copy Editor   Kathleen Green, Positively Proofed, Plano, TX
                                          info@PositivelyProofed.com

Design, art direction and production   Melissa Monogue, Back Porch Creative, Plano, TX
                                          info@BackPorchCreative.com

Introduction

*Difficulties are meant to rouse, not discourage.
The human spirit is to grow strong by conflict.*

William Ellery Channing

Conflict.

What do you think of when you hear that word? How does conflict make you feel? Many people say things like:

It makes me anxious and stressed out.

I feel frustrated when conflicts come up on my team because I know they will eat up time I'd planned for other work.

I lose my head and say things I later wish I hadn't.

I feel bad for my family because sometimes I take the stress from a work conflict home with me.

Dealing with conflict is the hardest thing about my job as a manager!

Sound familiar? Everyone struggles with how to deal with conflict. However, **the ability to effectively resolve conflict can be the difference between success or failure, job satisfaction or dissatisfaction, and a productive team or an apathetic one.**

It's estimated that more than 50 percent of managers' time is spent dealing with conflicts. *Fifty percent!* The cost of that time – not even considering lost sales and productivity – is enormous. Some experts estimate the cost of conflict is in the hundreds of thousands of dollars *per incident.*

You've probably experienced firsthand the realities and consequences of conflict in the workplace: the projects that are derailed; the energy that unresolved disagreements steal from you and your team; the negative impact on productivity; the missed targets, goals and deadlines. Just one incident can be so stress-inducing and unpleasant that it wipes out the whole day, evening and sometimes the entire week. One manager recently said, "When someone comes to me about a conflict, everything stops. I have to turn away from my work and help them. The time and energy it takes to step in and help them work something out is very draining. And the rest of the team is watching – they usually know about the conflict before it ever gets to me."

It's no wonder we see conflict as a huge pain in the neck!

But today, we're asking you to consider the possibility that conflict has gotten a bad rap, that maybe it's not as unpleasant as it seems. You see, **conflict is not inherently negative**. It's our interpretation of and response to conflict that is most often negative.

Conflict is inevitable – it's a normal aspect of human interaction. Conflict arises from unmet needs, unrecognized differences, and difficulties in coping with life changes and challenges – things that occur in offices and homes everywhere, every day. Conflict is simply a part of life.

Here is the good news: Conflict leads to progress! If handled calmly, skillfully and appropriately, conflict can move you and your team forward. **Conflict is an opportunity – an opportunity to create positive change.** Think about it. Most of the inventions, discoveries and technological advances made throughout history have been the result of humans developing solutions to conflicts, whether they were conflicts with other people, other nations, nature, our immediate surroundings, even the cells that make up our bodies. It's disagreements among scientists, explorers and philosophers that lead us to learn and understand more about our world and ourselves.

If necessity is the mother of invention,
then conflict is the father of positive change.

In business, conflict can lead to progress and opportunity as well. It offsets inertia, acts as a catalyst for an organization and its people to grow, and stimulates creativity and problem solving. In fact, too little conflict – settling for the status quo – can be just as harmful as too much. Without conflict, teams experience Group Think, in which team members become too similar in their mindset and outlook. This lack of diverse thought prevents dissenting opinions and innovative ideas from being shared and, ultimately, leads to poor decisions. Another effect of Group Think is that harmony becomes more important than wise decisions. No one in the group wants to "rock the boat," so decisions are made based on what feels good rather than what is best for the company or the customer.

High-performing managers understand that opportunity is often disguised as conflict.

The manager's role is not to avoid conflict, but to learn to manage it in a way that leverages its potential. *It all comes down to how you use it.* And that's precisely what this book is about: how to resolve conflict and create positive change in the process. The methods and techniques presented here will help you:

1. Prevent minor disagreements and differences from escalating into major conflicts

2. Effectively resolve the day-to-day conflicts that do come up

3. Enhance relationships

4. Coach your team members to resolve *their* conflicts faster and better, giving you one less thing to worry about!

Conflict will exist as long as people work and live together. Using the strategies in this book, you will approach conflict as an opportunity to change situations for the better – to create positive transformations – and to produce better outcomes for your team, your customers and your organization.

Contents

Take AIM!
The AIM Approach
to Resolving Conflict

*For every minute you remain angry,
you give up sixty seconds of peace of mind.*

Ralph Waldo Emerson

Let's face it: Dealing with conflict can be unpleasant. *But it doesn't have to be!* When faced with conflict – any kind of conflict, at work or at home – we tend to respond one of three ways:

1. Ignore It.

A natural response to conflict is to ignore it and hope it goes away. After all, who has the time and energy to take on conflict? But even when you think you're avoiding conflict, you're not. You're simply allowing other people or the passage of time to "respond" to the conflict for you. Consequently, you become a passive recipient of other people's choices and actions, for better or for worse.

When conflict is ignored, it doesn't go away. Quite the contrary; it often escalates. The 1-10-100 Rule illustrates the impact of allowing conflicts to persist. This rule states that the longer conflicts continue, the more expensive, time consuming and painful they will be to resolve. For example, if a conflict between two people is solved quickly and efficiently, it can be solved with the equivalent of one unit of time, money or resources. That same problem – if it's not addressed and spreads throughout a work group – will require the equivalent of *ten* units of time, money or resources to solve because more emotions and perceptions must be addressed. If the problem spreads throughout the organization or into the customer base, it will require at least *100* units of time, money or resources to solve. That is 100 times what it would have cost to solve the same conflict in the beginning!

When conflicts are ignored, molehills become mountains. It is less expensive and more effective to address conflicts before they escalate.

2. Respond emotionally or irrationally.

We frequently react to conflict illogically or unreasonably because we tend to take comments, situations and events personally. When we perceive disagreements or disputes as personal attacks, we're likely to reciprocate in kind, creating an ongoing cycle of resentment and confrontation.

Managers who overreact to conflict or handle it poorly may inadvertently punish those involved. Over time, distrust grows, relationships suffer and productivity drops off. The result is a toxic work environment.

3. Resolve it effectively.

For most of us, the mere thought of dealing with conflict brings a certain level of anxiety. But conflict can be resolved quickly, effectively and with less stress for all those involved.

In fact, you can learn to resolve conflicts in the workplace with ease by using an approach called AIM. AIM is an acronym:

Attitude – your positive beliefs and thoughts about the conflict

Intention – the outcome or result you'd like to achieve

Message – how you communicate your intention, both verbally and nonverbally

More than merely managing the negative effects of conflict, **AIM actually creates positive change.** AIM:

+ Resolves the conflict and enhances the relationship

+ Facilitates the best possible result for the organization

+ Ensures high performance and improves productivity

+ Leads to a better work environment

AIM works for everyone – whether you're an individual contributor or a CEO – and with all types of conflicts. However, there is one caveat: The AIM approach requires that you care (or are willing to start caring) about the dignity of all the people involved in the conflict. This can be tough, because there will be times when people treat *you* so unfairly that it's hard to want to treat *them* with respect. So why should you? Because resolving conflicts and disagreements will be more effective, easier, faster and less stressful.

Now, with that said, let's take aim!

Resolving conflict to create positive change is our goal. Let's AIM toward that target!

We all experience plenty of negative situations and people. The key is to be prepared to consciously respond to these negative inputs. Choosing to respond rather than react helps us positively orchestrate our attitudes…and our lives.

Lee J. Colan
Orchestrating Attitude

The A.I.M. Approach to Resolving Conflict

ATTITUDE

Whenever you're in conflict with someone, there is one factor that can make the difference between damaging your relationship and deepening it. That factor is attitude.

William James

Effectively resolving conflict begins with your attitude. Your attitude is powerful – there is a mountain of evidence that attitude influences all areas of life. Doctors confirm that the difference between those who survive serious illness or injury and those who don't is often the individual patient's attitude. In sports, coaches know that the team's attitude is a major piece of the game plan. Teachers see evidence every day that positive kids produce positive results. A Gallup Poll revealed that 90 percent of people say they are more productive at work when they are around positive people.

The impact of a positive attitude on your success is not just theory, but fact. You simply cannot create positive outcomes with a negative attitude.

Having a positive attitude about a conflict doesn't mean being idealistic or unrealistic. It means you believe that **it is at least possible to change the situation for the better**.

Whether you're personally involved in a conflict or you're helping others work through one, your attitude about the situation will significantly influence how it gets resolved.

Let's say one of your co-workers, Anthony, disagrees with your plans to implement a new customer service initiative. In addition, you've heard that he's badmouthed you and your idea to others. Just imagine the outcome of a discussion if you approach Anthony with thoughts like, "Anthony has way more clout with the boss than I do" or "Anthony is such a jerk. There's no way he's going to change his mind no matter how much sense I make." You would reek of negativism and that would play a huge role in the outcome of the discussion.

Consider, on the other hand, what might happen if you have a positive attitude going into the discussion: "I'm confident Anthony and I will have a productive discussion. We will agree on the best approach, and we'll have a pleasant interaction as well." Even if you are a skeptic, doesn't it make sense that a positive approach to conflict will result in a better outcome than a negative approach?

You are the creator of your thoughts; therefore, you are the creator of your attitude toward any conflict that comes your way. When you replace self-defeating or situation-defeating beliefs with realistic, optimistic thoughts, you open the door for good things to happen. Negative thoughts, on the other hand, will slam the door shut.

Sometimes, adjusting a pessimistic attitude will be easy: "Hey, wait a minute. I have lots of experience and insights about this decision to bring to the table." Other times, it will be more difficult, and you may have to stretch a bit to be upbeat. Let's face it, most of us have to work with people who we simply don't care for or who we constantly butt heads with. We're not suggesting that you convince yourself to be friends or that you even have to like them. A more positive yet still realistic attitude in this case would be to shift your feelings from dislike to tolerance, or to decide that you can have a civil working relationship despite your feelings.

It all comes down to a simple choice. You choose your attitude and, therefore, how quickly and easily conflicts will be resolved.

When it comes to Attitude...

It's not about being idealistic; it's about being positive.

Conflicts will occur in any relationship.
The ultimate test of a relationship is
to disagree but to respect the other person,
acknowledge your agreement to disagree,
and move forward without bitterness.

David Cottrell
Monday Morning Choices

The A.I.M. Approach to Resolving Conflict

 # INTENTION

> *You can have everything in life you want if you will just help other people get what they want.*
>
> Zig Ziglar

Few people would argue with our first point that a positive attitude increases the likelihood of a positive outcome. The next step in this conflict resolution process is to focus your positive energy and aim it in a specific direction. The tool for that focus is *intention*. Intention is the outcome or result you're hoping to achieve. That's easy – the outcome you're hoping to achieve is what *you* want, right? Not quite.

Resolving conflict is about reaching the best outcome for all concerned, whether that represents your idea, someone else's idea, some of both or neither.

Oftentimes in the midst of conflict we become entrenched in our "position." *Our* ideas, viewpoints and methods are, of course, *right*, and the other party's are, naturally, *wrong*. A key aspect of conflict resolution is your willingness to give up getting your way. That notion may seem counterintuitive at first. When you're at odds with someone, it often feels like one of you has to lose in order for the other one to win. Isn't that the way it is in sports? But **conflict isn't a contest!** It's not a duel where one side has to be left bleeding in the dirt.

Perhaps you believe that resolving conflict is about compromise, where each side gives up a little to gain something. No one loses and everyone benefits, right? Wrong! Many times a compromised result is a watered-down version of what both parties were seeking. But – and here's the catch – this outcome may not be the best decision for the company, your team or you. **Compromise is not necessarily a good thing.**

What if you were to approach conflict with the intention that no one has to lose and everyone can win? What if your intention was that everyone could benefit from the outcome without having to give something up in order to gain something? Ah, that's much more palatable than the winner/loser approach, and it even feels better than trying to figure out what you can afford to lose and what you have to hold onto in a compromise.

When your intention is to reach the best possible outcome for all involved, the very dynamics of the conflict immediately change.

In many organizations, the allocation of resources – money, time, people and equipment – is a common cause of conflict. Let's assume you are a leader in a large graphic design department. Many of the employees in this department have a solid knowledge base but need training to enhance their skills. A major project deadline is looming on the horizon, and you don't think the team possesses the necessary skills to effectively complete the project. You've been lobbying to invest the department's remaining $5,000 budget on an internal training effort that will give employees the needed skills. Yes, the project deadline will have to be pushed out, but you believe your strategy will solve the skill problem once and for all.

The other manager in the department, Luis, feels strongly that the budget dollars should be spent to bring in temporary external resources that possess the required skills to get the project completed on time. Luis believes that meeting project deadlines should be top priority, which means there isn't time to develop employees right now.

It may seem like your intention would be to get your way – to convince Luis that investing in employee development is the best way to spend the budget dollars. But when you step back, you realize that your ultimate goal is to do what is best for the company and that may not necessarily be represented by your idea. Given that you and Luis have butted heads a lot recently, perhaps you also want to be able to discuss the budget allocation in a way that won't leave you angry and with a headache. Here is the positive intention you develop:

> *My intention when I speak with Luis will be to reach an outcome that best serves the company and that our relationship will be improved as a result of the discussion.*

If you talk to Luis with this kind of positive intention, chances are he'll be open to hearing your views and you his. More than likely, together you will reach a decision that is best for the company while fostering a more cooperative relationship. Perhaps you think that's idealistic, but here's the bottom line: Approaching conflicts with genuine, noble, positive intentions not only creates better outcomes, but also leads to far less emotional and mental wear and tear on *you*. No more "fighting" for your idea or having to live with a compromise that doesn't really meet anyone's needs.

Clarifying your intention is an often-ignored aspect of managing conflict. The more focused your intention, the more likely you are to achieve it. If you don't take a few minutes to think about the specific outcome you want, there will be no focus and the discussion will wander all over the place. Before going into any conflict resolution discussion, write down your intention. This will help you crystallize your thoughts and honestly examine what it is you want. You know you're looking for a positive result, but positive for whom or for what? When the conversation is over…

✦ **What actions do you want to occur?**

✦ **What do you want to feel?**

✦ **What do you want the other party(ies) to feel?**

Consider a typical real-world challenge: You've been having an ongoing disagreement with your next-door neighbor about who should fix the common fence between your yards. You've adjusted your attitude about the situation and have decided it's possible to have a positive outcome. Now it's time to think about your intention. After all, you could just repair the fence yourself. But you actually want more than a fixed fence – you want your neighbor to share in the repair. You also want to have a pleasant talk and a better relationship with your neighbor so that it will be easier to solve neighbor-related problems together in the future. Here is the intention you write down:

My intention when I speak with my neighbor is an outcome in which the fence is fixed in a way that serves my needs as well as his and that our relationship will be improved as a result.

Taking a moment to clarify and write down your intention will pay huge dividends in the form of better outcomes and better relationships.

When it comes to Intention...

It's not about *your* win; it's about *the* win.

If you have trouble identifying your intention, the following is an "all-purpose" intention that can lead to more productive outcomes in most every situation and conflict:

My intention as I approach this conflict is to achieve the best possible outcome for all concerned and that my relationship with those involved will be improved.

First Impressions Really Do Count

Remember the adage, "It only takes seconds to make a first impression"? The same is true with conflict resolution. How you first attempt to convey your intention can cause the other person to feel:

- Defensive and want to mount a counterattack;

- Embarrassed or guilty and want to retreat;

- Supported and want to engage in constructive resolution.

Those first few seconds of a conflict discussion are the most critical because that's when the other person – right or wrong – judges your intention. If your positive intention is clear from the outset, you're much more likely to have a successful outcome.

The A.I.M. Approach to Resolving Conflict

 # MESSAGE

So you've committed to having a positive attitude about a particular conflict. You've even changed your original intention from getting your way, or perhaps giving in, to resolving the disagreement in a way that is best for all and leaves the relationship intact. The third step is to express your message – to effectively communicate your true intention and a whole lot more – so the other party will believe you, shift their attitude and open up to possible solutions.

Your message is delivered with both verbal and nonverbal communication. We'll begin with the nonverbal message because this is actually the most crucial part.

The Nonverbal Message

What you do speaks so loud I cannot hear what you say.

Ralph Waldo Emerson

Numerous studies have discovered that up to 85 percent of all communication is nonverbal. We think the actual number is even higher!

Picture, if you will, an individual sitting on one side of a room. He is slouched over, looking down with a frown on his face. If he said to you in a low, depressing tone, "I'm so happy," would you believe him? Of course not. On the other side of the room is another person. She is sitting ramrod straight with a huge smile on her face. Her eyes are wide open, and she seems to be overflowing with energy. She shouts, "I'M SO UNHAPPY!" Which do you believe – her nonverbal or verbal message?

Your nonverbal behavior conveys more than your verbal message.

Without question, your nonverbal, physical messages speak louder and more clearly than your words. With the AIM approach, the words you use, while important, are not the most important aspect. In conflict management training, participants often want to get immediately to the "script" – the actual words they will say. But **if your attitude, intention and nonverbal message are not in alignment, what you say won't matter much at all.**

Fortunately, you don't have to "learn" how to manage your nonverbal behavior. Just believe in and commit to your intention. Is it really that simple? Yes. If your intention is noble, authentic and sincere, the nonverbals will take care of themselves. The majority of the meaning of your message will be conveyed by your behavior – posture, gestures, eyes and tone – and you'll have a strong chance of the receiver "hearing" the message you intend.

Some people physically show they care by leaning forward, others by leaning back. When you genuinely care about the relationship and want to reach the best outcome, your body will respond accordingly, and it will be real and perceived as sincere by the other party. If I sat across from you with three typical "closed" nonverbal indications – arms folded, sitting back, legs crossed – yet my intentions were noble, you likely wouldn't perceive me as closed or angry.

If you truly believe your positive intentions, your behavior will naturally reflect those intentions.

The Verbal Message

> *The great enemy of clear language is insincerity.*
> George Orwell

To this point, our discussion has centered on your role in resolving conflicts – your attitude, intentions and nonverbal behaviors. However, by definition, a conflict involves more than one party. That's why resolving conflict takes EFFORT – because there are always other attitudes, other intentions and other messages to consider. EFFORT is another acronym used to describe the process of effectively delivering your verbal message. Let's look at each step in detail:

Explain your intentions. Add any information that may help the other party see and hear your sincerity. Before you state your intention, ask yourself:

+ *Will what I am about to say serve to resolve the issue?* (If not, then revisit the chapters on Attitude and Intention.)

+ *Will what I am about to say serve to maintain or improve my relationship with this person?* (If not, then revisit the chapters on Attitude and Intention.)

To create positive change, it's necessary to understand the conflict from the other party's perspective. Invite the other party to explain by asking a simple question: "What do you want out of this discussion?" If you've sincerely spoken your intention of wanting what is best for all concerned and your nonverbal behaviors are in sync with that message, they will likely be open to sharing their intentions as well.

Find common ground. Identify as many areas as possible where all parties are in agreement or your interests are the same. Start with broad concepts such as, "We both want what is best for the customer" or "As a team, we want to work in a more positive, productive, less stressful environment." Then continue with more specific areas you have in common. Searching for and emphasizing areas of agreement is a powerful way to move a conflict forward.

Flexibility is crucial. Commit to maintaining an open mind. Without that commitment, you're more likely to fall back into a my-way-or-the-highway perspective or to try to convince the other person your position is the best one. Being flexible means staying in exploratory mode, searching for the best possible resolution, which may or may not be the solution you had in mind to begin with. Of course, you can't control the other person's flexibility, but your willingness to remain flexible garners trust with others.

Options. Brainstorm potential solutions to resolve the conflict in a way that will satisfy all parties. Don't get hooked into just three possibilities: your way, the other person's way or a compromise. Explore various options to achieve the objectives you have in common. Remember that your team members are usually the most familiar with the challenge or issue at hand. Front-line employees often know better than anyone how to solve problems and can frequently provide options that may not be readily apparent to you. So listen to their input with respect and a nonjudgmental attitude.

Resolve the conflict. First, ask the other party(ies): "Do you think I've listened to your concerns with an open mind? Have we considered everyone's viewpoint and all the important information?" Then decide on the solution(s) that best addresses your common interests. Finally, confirm that everyone can support the resolution. With AIM and EFFORT, you'll be pleasantly surprised that most conflicts do, in fact, get resolved.

Take action. Often we are so exhausted after dealing with a conflict that once we reach agreement, we call it a day. Or, next steps are generally mentioned during the discussion, but aren't clarified with respect to the "who, what and when." If you don't end the discussion with a precise understanding and agreement about the specific actions that will follow, you may be setting yourself up for future misunderstandings and a rehashing of the same issue.

Now, let's look at an example to illustrate how you can use EFFORT to resolve conflicts in the workplace. You are a manager and Tanya is a member of your team, and the two of you are having a disagreement about her performance review. Tanya believes she should receive an "exceeds expectations," while you believe her performance only met expectations.

Explain

You: *Tanya, my intent with this discussion is to be sure we both leave believing that we understand each other's point of view and that we can move forward in a positive manner. What would you like to see come out of this discussion?*

Tanya: *Well, obviously, I want my review changed to "exceeds expectations."*

You: *I understand, and it's also important to me that my reviews are perceived as fair.*

Tanya: *I want the same thing – a fair review – and I don't think I got one.*

Find

You: *So we have something in common already. We both want the review to be fair. Is there anything else we agree on?*

Tanya: *Like you said, I want to go back to work feeling positive ... I don't want to be upset while talking to customers on the phone. I just want to feel good about what I do, and I think I do a good job.*

You: *So we both want to be able to get back to work and not have this issue hanging over our heads. We both want a resolution that we can live with. Is that right?*

Tanya: *Yes.*

Flexibility

You: *Okay. I'd like you to explain why you believe you exceeded expectations, and then I will explain why I believe you met expectations. As you probably know, it's rare for a manager to change a review. If I've missed some facts that show why the* *review should be changed, then I'm open to doing so. I just ask that you give my facts the same consideration. Agreed?*

Tanya: *Yes.*

You and Tanya proceed to review each other's supporting evidence.

Options

You: *Based on what each of us just shared, I see a few options for how we can proceed. I still believe that "meets expectations" is a fair evaluation. At the same time, I also see the opportunity to clarify what it will take for you to exceed expectations on your next review. It seems to me that we disagree the most about those activities that I see as part of your job and you see as going above and beyond normal job responsibilities. I'm wondering if a clearer set of expectations and a development plan would help. Another option is for you to talk to HR if you still believe the evaluation isn't fair. Any other options that you see?*

Tanya: *Yes. I'd like some time overnight to think about what you said. I have a hard time reacting to things on the spot.*

You: *Okay. How about we both think about this discussion and meet again tomorrow morning?*

Tanya: *Okay.*

The next day, the conversation continues:

You: *Now that we've both had some time to reflect, what thoughts do you have on moving forward?*

Tanya: *I know we agree on a lot, but I guess we really do disagree about what "meets" and "exceeds" mean.*

You: *Yes, with the reduction in workforce we experienced earlier this year, we all have to step up and do more as part of our jobs. That includes me. Changes in our industry are fast and furious these days.*

Tanya: *And in order to be fair to employees, I think management has to do a better job of clarifying the new expectations. I think we should meet at least once a quarter to review expectations so I have a chance to understand what it will take to exceed expectations in the future.*

You: *That's a great suggestion. I agree. And what about this evaluation? Let's go back to the intentions we both shared. Do you believe we now understand each other's point of view?*

Tanya: *Yes, I do.*

Resolution

You: *I do, too. Initially, your intention was to have the review changed to "exceeds expectations." Based on the criteria that were in place during the review period, even after hearing your evidence, I believe "meets expectations" is fair. And, I agree that we both need to have more clarity about the criteria going forward. Given that, can you sign this evaluation and feel positive about it?*

Tanya: *Well, I'm still not happy about it, but I understand where you're coming from. And knowing things will be clearer in the future, I'm willing to sign it.*

Take Action

You: *Okay, so we agree that we will both now sign the evaluation. In addition, I'll begin working on a specific plan to outline what level of performance will meet expectations and what it* *will take to exceed expectations as best we can determine now. I'll get it to you by the end of the week, and then we'll meet quarterly to check progress. Now, are you sure you can move forward in a positive manner – something we both agreed was important?*

Tanya: *Yes.*

You: *I'm glad we were able to have a good, honest discussion, resolve this issue and have something positive – better clarification of expectations – come out of it. Thanks.*

Conflict resolution discussions rarely follow a set, step-by-step sequence. You may be talking about Options and find that you need to go back and Explain your intentions again. And, of course, being Flexible should happen throughout the exchange. EFFORT is not intended to be a rigid, linear process, but rather a template for an effective conflict resolution discussion.

As you can see, handling a conflict well takes EFFORT. *Not* managing a conflict takes even more effort, creates more stress and usually leads to more conflicts. Your *mindset* is crucial to the process. **Without Attitude and Intention, the Message and all your EFFORT will be for naught**. Proper AIM dramatically increases your chances of hitting the target – resolving the conflict with the best possible outcome, enhancing the relationship and creating positive change.

When it comes to the Message...

It's not just about the words; it's about the sincerity behind the words.

10 Ways to Make Sure a
Conflict Resolution Discussion FAILS
(What NOT to do)

1. Avoid the conflict at all costs – maybe the problem will just go away.

2. React on the spot without thinking.

3. Take things personally.

4. If someone is highly emotional, tell the person to "calm down."

5. When attacked, attack back.

6. Handle the conflict via e-mail!

7. Say the "right" words without being sincere.

8. Push the discussion no matter how upset you or the other person gets.

9. Focus only on your interests and forget the interests of others.

10. Jump into conflict resolution discussions without adjusting your Attitude and writing your Intention.

You Can't Resolve A Conflict Face-to-Face

Electric communication will never be a substitute for the face of someone who with their soul encourages another person to be brave and true.

Charles Dickens

Many managers lead people who are not in the same building, town or even country. Distance certainly doesn't eliminate conflicts. In fact, it can create more challenges when conflicts arise. Because so much of our message is communicated through nonverbal behaviors, physical separation makes conveying our intention more difficult.

There is one hard rule – and we do mean rule (no exceptions!) – for conveying your message when conflicts can't be handled in person:

NEVER attempt to resolve a conflict via e-mail!

A *USA Today* survey revealed that 80 percent of adults find it easy to misinterpret an e-mail sender's intended tone. We've counseled more people than we can count about conflicts that were either created or made worse due to the use of e-mail. When nonverbal behaviors such as body language, facial expressions and voice tone can't be seen or heard, recipients have no choice but to assume the meaning behind the words. And more often than not, people lean toward negative rather than positive assumptions. Don't put people in a situation where *they* must decide *your* intention by guessing at the nonverbal behaviors accompanying your words.

So how do you resolve remote conflicts? First, prepare the same way you would with a face-to-face meeting – take AIM and use EFFORT. Then…

Pick up the phone and have a conversation, live and in real time!

While conducting a sensitive discussion via the phone is not the first choice, it is our best choice when we can't be face-to-face. It still allows you to be real and sincere with those on the other end. Yes, they will miss your facial expressions and body language, but they will hear your tone of voice, and you theirs.

Especially when using the phone, you must effectively convey the positive intentions behind your words. Here are some tips for doing just that:

+ Pay extra attention to your tone of voice to be sure you sound as you intend.

+ Eliminate distractions that could take your focus away from the conversation (people will hear that you're not fully present and could interpret this as you not caring about them and/or the issue at hand, especially if they hear the clicking of the keys as you check your e-mail!).

✦ Check in with the other person frequently to be sure your intention is being heard correctly.

✦ Listen for the other person's nonverbal messages that are inconsistent with what is spoken, such as hesitations, uncertain tone, etc.

Is resolving remote conflicts more difficult? Yes. Impossible? Definitely not. Remember to keep your AIM focused and give it a bit more EFFORT.

When it comes to long-distance conflict...

It's not about e-mail; it's about being real!

What To Do When...

You're Confronted with a Highly Emotional Response

Where we have strong emotions, we're liable to fool ourselves.

Carl Sagan

Highly emotional conflicts deserve special mention as they call for special skills. Given the very nature of conflict, it's reasonable to expect that the people involved will have some level of emotion. But strong emotions cloud our judgment and make resolving conflicts more difficult. A strong emotion is not always loud, obvious anger. Sometimes it's a different kind of intense reaction such as quiet anger or clamming up or tears.

When a simple discussion suddenly turns emotional or you're minding your own business and someone confronts you in anger, you must first manage the emotions before you can manage the conflict. Chances are the other person isn't going to listen to your intention until s/he believes you understand that s/he's upset. Acknowledge the emotion by using what we call the "I got it" message … quickly!

Imagine that Ryan, one of your team members, walks up, slaps a piece of paper on your desk and says in an angry voice, "I can't believe you put Terry – and not me – on the agenda to discuss the Riverside project. I did all the work on it. He hardly knows anything about it."

Before you offer your noble intention, you need to let Ryan know you realize this is a big deal to him: "Ryan, I can see you're upset about this, so it must be very important to you."

If said with sincerity, this is all you probably need to say for Ryan to hear that you got the message. Don't expect him to immediately calm down … because that takes time. But when you recognize his feelings, he'll likely take his emotions down a notch or two, at least to the point where you can have a productive discussion.

Acknowledge the other person's emotions before offering your message.

Sometimes, the level of emotional reaction is highly disproportionate to the situation or issue at hand. Here's an example: You come home from work, enter your bedroom and see your spouse picking up your socks and dirty clothes from the floor. Upon seeing you, s/he yells, "I'm sick and tired of picking up after you! I feel like I live with a child!"

Clearly, your spouse is emotional … to put it mildly. With this high level of emotion, the "I got it" message typically isn't enough to change the tenor of the conversation. Imagine saying, "Okay, I can see you're very upset about the socks." Your spouse would likely yell back, "You think?" or "Well, aren't you a genius!"

The "I got it" message doesn't work here – even when spoken with sincere intentions – because your spouse actually isn't angry about the socks. When there is an unusually high level of emotion attached to a seemingly small problem or situation, there is typically a larger, more significant problem that exists. In many cases, the other person believes one of his/her core needs or principles has been neglected. Most of us share basic personal needs such as appreciation, fairness and respect, and it's often a smaller issue (like dirty socks on the floor) that symbolizes an attack on these highly regarded needs. In other words, **it's not about the socks!**

Look beyond the situation at hand, search for the bigger issue and take your best guess as to what's really going on. Think about it ... what possible larger issues could leaving your socks on the floor trigger in your spouse? Perhaps s/he's asked you to pick up your clothes a hundred times before and feels you don't *listen* to her/him. Or maybe your spouse feels *unappreciated* or *disrespected* by you. You might say, "From the way you're reacting, I'm thinking this anger is not about the socks – it's about something bigger. I'm sensing you may feel that I don't appreciate all you do around here."

If you've correctly identified the bigger issue, find common ground by sincerely letting the person know that you agree with her/his concern. With your spouse you might say, "I do appreciate all that you do. I never want you to feel like I take you for granted." This usually reduces the intensity of the emotion and paves the way for a more fruitful discussion. If your guess was incorrect, you may still get a helpful response. Your spouse might say, "No, it's not that I don't feel appreciated. I think you just don't care about what is important to me." Now you know the real issue and can deal with it openly.

When emotions run high, the most visible problem is not the first problem to be addressed. Take your best guess and address the BIGGER issue.

The it's-not-about-the-socks phenomenon applies in organizations as well. When someone at work goes ballistic about a seemingly small issue, you can bet the person is actually upset about something larger. For example, you're in the midst of a disagreement with a peer, Mercedes, about how to respond to an internal client's request. The discussion is civil until Mercedes suddenly explodes and says, "What's the point in talking to you? You always get your way anyway!"

Shocked at her reaction, you quickly realize that "it's not about the socks" and there must be something else going on here. You respond, "Wow, Mercedes, I didn't expect that reaction about this issue. Is there something else going on that has you upset? You said I always get my way. Are you angry because during the last two team meetings, my ideas for the redesign were approved and yours weren't?"

Mercedes replies, "It's just that sometimes I feel there is no point in disagreeing with you. You have Devon's ear, so you always seem to get what you want." The underlying issue is now on the table. You resolve that conflict first; then return to the client problem and, with emotions out of the way, quickly find a solution.

When strong emotions are involved, always address the emotion and/or its cause first. Sometimes a statement recognizing the situation is all you need to reduce the emotional intensity. But when someone reacts to a small situation in a big way, remember that the conflict before you is masking a larger issue.

When it comes to high emotion...

It's not about "the socks"; it's about something bigger.

What To Do When...

You're Caught in a Surprise Attack

Remember not only to say the right thing in the right place, but far more difficult still, to leave unsaid the wrong thing at the tempting moment.

Benjamin Franklin

There are times when conflict sneaks up on you and catches you so off guard that you don't have time to take AIM. When you're blindsided, angry or just too off balance to be effective, try using one of these strategies:

1. **Ask for a time-out.** Take the shortest amount of time necessary to allow you to regroup and approach the conflict in a constructive manner. How you ask for a time-out is the key to making it work. Here again, if your intention is to do the best for all concerned, offer that as your reason for wanting a break.

   For example, there you are, minding your own business when a co-worker suddenly confronts you and accuses you of undermining him because you changed a deadline. You might say:

I can see you're upset with me about the changed deadline. Your response has really taken me by surprise. I'd like a few minutes to get my thoughts together. I don't want to avoid the discussion; I just want to postpone it until I can discuss the situation in a way that will lead to a productive outcome. Can I come to your area in about 15 minutes?

If he isn't willing to postpone, use active listening skills while he is venting to help you better understand the issue and return to a more focused state.

2. **Use the "best friend" technique** when you suspect that suggesting a time-out will only add fuel to the fire. This is a mindset strategy. Think of a person in your life whom you trust completely to stand for your best interests – perhaps your best friend. This should be a person you care so deeply about that, if s/he were upset with you, your emotions would be that of concern and caring rather than anger or fear. Then, pretend that the other person involved in the conflict is your trusted friend and show him/her the same consideration you'd give your friend. If you do this for only a minute or two, your feelings of being attacked will dissipate, and your care and concern will be felt by the other person.

When you don't have time to take AIM at a conflict, try a time-out or the "best friend" technique until you can compose yourself and return to the conflict resolution techniques you've learned.

When it comes to surprise attacks...

It's not about jumping in; it's about stepping back.

What To Do When...

You Sense the Potential for Violence

You can't shake hands with a clenched fist.

Indira Gandhi

As with most effective solutions, there are exceptions to AIM and EFFORT – situations when dealing with a conflict may not be the wisest course of action. If there is any hint of violence or even potential violence, get away from the person immediately and get help. This is NOT the time to offer your intention, consider the bigger issue or think of your best friend. It's time to leave!

If you sense violence, stop the discussion and get to safety.

In order for the concepts and techniques we've discussed to be effective, a somewhat rational state of mind must exist. When someone is in a violent state, chemical reactions inside the person's body make it nearly impossible for him/her to have a reasonable discussion. Your objective is to get to safety, not to be an effective communicator – unless your job is in law enforcement!

When it comes to violent conflicts...

It's not about resolution; it's about safety.

Preventative Maintenance

The people to fear are not those who disagree with you,
but those who disagree with you
and are too cowardly to let you know.

Joe Moore

If used on a regular basis, "preventative maintenance" can keep small disagreements from becoming larger conflicts. This is when an ounce of prevention can be worth several pounds of your favorite headache remedy! Preventative maintenance means you are constantly watching and listening for people's reactions and getting potential conflicts out in the open before negative thoughts begin to fester and grow.

Assume that you're in a meeting, and you ask one of your product managers to arrange a meeting with the sales team for next week. You notice that another team member, William, seems to have a negative reaction: He opens his eyes wide as if surprised, shakes his head and then shrugs and looks down. All this happens in about two seconds. Most people at the meeting don't even see it.

A few notice but decide that since he didn't say anything, it must not be important.

But dealing with such nonverbal reactions when they occur can often prevent future conflicts. If the people at the meeting are fairly comfortable with each other, you can state what you observed: "William, I couldn't help but notice that you seemed surprised and perhaps even uncomfortable when I suggested we meet with the sales team next week. Your input is valuable, and I'm wondering if you have information we should know about before we move forward."

As with AIM and EFFORT, your intent is crucial. If you put people on the spot, they'll clam up even more. After all, something stopped them from being direct in the first place. On the other hand, if you express that you sincerely want to explore their concerns, they'll be more likely to open up. If discussing such an issue in a group setting isn't appropriate or comfortable, speak with the person alone immediately after the meeting with the same language and intent.

In our example above, William proceeds to explain (in a frustrated tone) that preparing for and having a meeting with the sales team would take valuable time away from the new product launch that he understands to be the team's number one priority. You thank William for sharing his concern and then solicit the team's input on how to adjust resources and develop a plan to achieve both goals. Had you ignored William's reaction, you likely would have ended up with an angry, aggravated employee who was unsure of his priorities and therefore might not meet your expectations.

Take note and take action when someone's nonverbal behaviors don't match what they say.

Some people don't like this tip. A manager once told us, "If someone tells me he is fine with a decision, but his nonverbal behavior suggests something else, that's his problem. It's his responsibility to get his issues out on the table. I don't believe my job is to baby people. I take them at their word."

Sure, that is how it *should* work. In a perfect world, everyone would say what they mean and not have to resort to nonverbal hints about what they're really thinking or feeling. But that's not the world we live in at work or at home. For a variety of reasons, people often don't feel they can be direct and share their concerns up front. Have *you* ever felt uncomfortable telling your boss something or giving him/her some kind of feedback? We've all been there.

When people think that it's not safe to share their thoughts openly, they send indirect messages, hoping others will pick up on them and inquire. It's in *your* best interest as a leader to get to the root of potential problems. Addressing inconsistent verbal and nonverbal messages is preventative in nature. If you fail to notice – or notice but fail to do anything about your observation – resentment will build, the disagreement will grow into a conflict or your efforts will be subverted in some way. In the end, you are the one most negatively affected if your employees don't give their full effort to a decision. Dealing with indirect messages up front allows for more options, greater efficiency and builds trust as you demonstrate that you care about your people.

When it comes to preventing conflict...

It's not about what people say; it's about what they *want* to say.

10 Ways to Keep a Conflict from Escalating

1. Get all the facts and clearly identify the problem.

2. Encourage people to challenge the status quo early so that all different opinions are on the table from the outset.

3. Do your best to see the positive in situations and people.

4. Be willing to listen and consider all viewpoints, especially those you disagree with.

5. When others explain their intention and viewpoints, summarize and paraphrase to confirm understanding.

6. Look for common ground in any difficult situation.

7. When possible, resolve one issue at a time.

8. Deal with the molehills before they become mountains!

9. Only send and respond to e-mails that are informational in nature. If there is any hint of disagreement, meet in person or pick up the phone.

10. Watch and listen for inconsistencies between people's words and their nonverbal behaviors and encourage them to voice their concerns.

Sharpening
Your AIM

The skill to do comes from the doing.

Cicero

This book has given you the knowledge and skills you need to effectively resolve conflict and create positive change. However, as Cicero wisely pointed out, your skill in dealing with conflict can only be improved by … dealing with conflict.

Learning how to successfully manage conflict is much like learning how to successfully drive a car. When you learn how to drive, you read the driver's handbook or take a course at a driving school. Does reading the book or completing the course mean you're a safe and proficient driver? Not necessarily. While you would be better *prepared* to be a good driver, you can't become a good driver until you get actual driving experience.

Likewise, this book has prepared you to resolve conflicts in the workplace in a safe and successful manner. But to become proficient, you need "behind-the-wheel training," so to speak. There simply is no substitute for doing. We learn by doing.

Here are some things you can do to gain actual experience in resolving conflict and improve your proficiency:

- ✦ Practice AIM and EFFORT in safe, low-risk situations … at first to gain confidence before tackling tougher situations.
- ✦ Reread this handbook periodically, honing in on a different section each time, and use the summary on page 52 to reinforce key concepts and techniques *before* entering into a conflict resolution discussion.
- ✦ Learn more about conflict resolution programs offered by co-author Ilayne J. Geller, by contacting her at Ilayne@CornerStoneLeadership.com.
- ✦ Identify coaches – people in your life who are skilled at dealing with conflict – and ask them to mentor you.

To be successful as a manager, you have no alternative but to address conflicts. The question is, how big of a role should you play in team members' problems? You can certainly play the lead role, but you may soon find you've become a convenient corporate dumping ground for everyone's issues. On the other hand, if you're completely uninvolved, you'll eventually be surrounded by mountains that grew from molehills.

Management is often a balancing act. You must walk the fine line of knowing when and how far to insert yourself into any given conflict. For greater success, help your team resolve its own conflicts. Start by proving to them that this approach works. Set the example. Demonstrate your ease and comfort with the techniques you've learned. Observing your new skills, others will take note of the positive changes.

Then, teach team members the AIM approach so they can use it themselves. Share this book with your team or provide copies for every team member. Coach them in the process as conflicts and disagreements arise. When your team is confident they can resolve conflicts, your involvement will be required less often.

Teach your team how to effectively resolve conflicts for themselves. Then be a coach and cheerleader.

Just imagine how your professional life and work environment would change for the better if your co-workers, team members, even your boss, possessed the same knowledge and skills you've learned in this book and had the same goal of resolving conflict and creating positive change. For instance:

- ✦ People throughout the organization would approach conflict discussions with constructive intention, knowing that something good will come from them.

- ✦ Everyone would be confident in knowing how to address the disagreements that inevitably crop up in the workplace.

- ✦ Team members would resolve conflicts with each other instead of dragging you into the fray.

- ✦ Managers would note when heated discussions are "not about the socks" and search for the bigger cause of disproportionate emotional reactions.

Will it happen overnight? No. Most organizations and teams that have experienced a great deal of conflict must rewrite their "history." It takes time to earn trust and rebuild relationships. But when you start with a positive attitude and noble intentions, your conflicts will be resolved quicker and with less stress on your soul. Given that these two elements are completely within your control, you can't help but succeed in creating positive change for your team, your organization and yourself.

Conflict Resolution Summary

Take AIM at the conflict:

Attitude – Is my attitude toward the situation and the people involved positive?

Intention – Is my intention to find the best possible outcome for all concerned and enhance the relationship? My intention is (write your intention below):

Message – Am I prepared to express my intention sincerely, both verbally and nonverbally?

Give the discussion my best EFFORT:

Explain – Sincerely share my intention and encourage others to share theirs.

Find – Find common ground, as many areas of agreement as possible.

Flexibility – Keep an open mind and be ready to consider any number of possibilities, including a solution that's not mine.

Options – Brainstorm potential solutions to resolve the conflict in a way that will satisfy all parties.

Resolve – Decide on a solution that addresses common interests and that everyone can support.

Take Action – Leave the discussion with a clear understanding of future actions, including the "who, what and when."

Remember...

It's not about being idealistic;
it's about being positive.

It's not about *your* win; it's about *the* win.

It's not just about the words; it's about the
sincerity behind the words.

In long-distance conflict,
it's not about e-mail; it's about being real!

With high emotion, it's not about "the socks";
it's about something bigger.

When caught off guard, it's not about
jumping in; it's about stepping back.

With potential violence, it's not about
resolution; it's about safety.

In preventing conflict, it's not about what
people say; it's about what they *want* to say.

Bottom line...

It's not about letting conflict manage you;
it's about *you* managing conflict.

It's about taking AIM, making an EFFORT
and creating positive change.

Recommended Reading

The Manager's Coaching Handbook is a practical guide to improve performance from your superstars, middle stars and falling stars. $9.95

The Manager's Communication Handbook will allow you to connect with employees and create the understanding, support and acceptance critical to your success. $9.95

Monday Morning Leadership is David Cottrell's best-selling book. It offers unique encouragement and direction that will help you become a better manager, employee and person. $14.95

Monday Morning Choices is about success … how to achieve it, keep it and enjoy it … by making better choices. $19.95

175 Ways to Get More Done in Less Time has 175 really good suggestions that will help you get things done faster … usually better. $9.95

Orchestrating Attitude translates the incomprehensible into the actionable. It cuts through the clutter to deliver inspiration and application so you can orchestrate your attitude … and your success. $9.95

The Manager's Conflict Resolution Handbook PowerPoint Presentation

Introduce *The Manager's Conflict Resolution Handbook* to your organization with this complete, cost-effective companion piece. All the main concepts and ideas in the book are reinforced in this professionally designed, downloadable presentation. It even includes speaking notes to make it a turnkey presentation for you! Use the presentation for kickoff meetings, training sessions, brown bag lunches or as a follow-up development tool. Downloadable at www.CornerStoneLeadership.com. **$99.95**

Visit www.CornerStoneLeadership.com for additional books and resources.

YES! Please send me extra copies of
The Manager's Conflict Resolution Handbook

1-99 copies $9.95   100-999 copies $8.95   1000+ copies $7.95

| *The Manager's Conflict Resolution Handbook* | _____ copies X _____ | = $ _____ |

The Manager's Conflict Resolution Handbook **Companion Resources**

| PowerPoint® Presentation (downloadable) | _____ copies X $99.95 | = $ _____ |

Recommended Reading

The Manager's Coaching Handbook	_____ copies X $9.95	= $ _____
The Manager's Communication Handbook	_____ copies X $9.95	= $ _____
Monday Morning Leadership	_____ copies X $14.95	= $ _____
Monday Morning Choices	_____ copies X $19.95	= $ _____
175 Ways to Get More Done in Less Time	_____ copies X $9.95	= $ _____
Orchestrating Attitude	_____ copies X $9.95	= $ _____

	Shipping & Handling	$ _____
	Subtotal	$ _____
	Sales Tax (8.25%-TX Only)	$ _____
	Total (U.S. Dollars Only)	**$ _____**

Shipping and Handling Charges

Total $ Amount	Up to $49	$50-$99	$100-$249	$250-$1199	$1200-$2999	$3000+
Charge	$7	$9	$16	$30	$80	$125

Name _____ Job Title _____

Organization _____ Phone _____

Shipping Address _____ Fax _____

Billing Address _____ E-mail _____
(required when ordering PowerPoint® Presentation)

City _____ State _____ ZIP _____

❏ Please invoice (Orders over $200) Purchase Order Number (if applicable) _____

Charge Your Order: ❏ MasterCard   ❏ Visa   ❏ American Express

Credit Card Number _____ Exp. Date _____

Signature _____

❏ Check Enclosed (Payable to: CornerStone Leadership)

Fax	**Mail**	**Phone**
972.274.2884	P.O. Box 764087	888.789.5323
	Dallas, TX 75376	

www.**CornerStoneLeadership**.com

Thank you for reading *The Manager's Conflict Resolution Handbook!*
We hope it has assisted you in your quest for
personal and professional growth.

CornerStone Leadership is committed to providing new
and enlightening products to organizations worldwide.
Our mission is to fuel knowledge with practical resources
that will accelerate your team's productivity,
success and job satisfaction!

Best wishes for your continued success.

Leadership Institute

www.CornerStoneLeadership.com

Start a crusade in your organization —
have the courage to learn, the vision to lead,
and the passion to share.